TABLE OF CONTENTS

INTRODUCTION

Are you stuck at figuring out a new business idea? Do you want advice on some quick, simple and fun ways to generate ideas? Are you thinking about your interests and hobbies and how to do what you love (career or study path)?

It is clear that there is an abundance of literature focused on developing the ideas, writing business plans or offering career advice, but there is a very limited supply of material to help those who are on the very early stage of the ideation process. Is it you?

This book welcomes you on a quest to find your own path, be it a new career or your business, based on your passions, hobbies and interests.

Happiness comes when you are happy with your inner self. Hence the realisation of who you are and what are your own aspirations was at the base of this idea generation journey.

More than 40 business titles were researched to compile this illustrated material on different creative techniques following a logical flow of learning more about yourself, looking and evaluating different options, sharing and connecting with others, shaping your ideas and preparing your plan. The titles listed in Bibliography are also reviewed at www.eviljoy.com, so should you wish to read more about a particular subject, please have a look.

Welcome on this engaging quest for new ideas and let our evil Joy, Robin and Penguin help you to make it fun and useful!

CHAPTER 1. ABOUT IDEAS

Oh, I wish I had that breakthrough business idea!

I keep trying to develop a brilliant business idea, but I seem to have no clue at all. Does it sound familiar?

Many are researching and thinking, but never actually creating.

What are my odds of starting the business?
Where do I start?
Is there a room in business for a regular sort of person?

Let's explore.

Remember those moments when you felt stuck, you tried even harder and there was nothing coming as a result at all? You felt frustrated.

We are discussing new idea generation here, but do you agree that in fact all knowledge workers need inspiration, creativity to constantly generate new ideas and innovate?

Books on entrepreneurship offer advice. Many of them are focusing on exact rules how to start a business from a management standpoint (legal, accounting, balance sheets, etc). Yet almost none actually tell how to generate that initial idea.

This quest was created to fill that void.

Have you tried some of those business books that look like encyclopedia?
They are quite large and boring manuals.

Now think about fiction
- it has conflicts, emotions and a lot of unknown.

Startups have that too, why to strip the entrepreneurial journey from fun?
Let's only add some more fun to it!

How about you meet Robin, little evil Joy and Penguin now?

They are entrepreneurs. They represent different sides of us - treat is as a truth or exaggeration, that is for you to decide.

Joy is a little Evil who depicts our risk-taking and somewhat gambling side. Think about things you have never told, something that makes you quietly scream

English Robin is on the quest to help others and change the world.

He is quite impulsive and very driven when it comes to social enterprises and new businesses.

Clever Penguin is a mastermind, an expert and also a good friend.

He is analytical, reads like a bookworm and scans through a lot of innovations. He is very opinionated.

We hear about creativity since Roman and Greek times, it appeared as either divine entities that help artists or as daemons.

Books portray it as a magical blessing that suddenly happens one day. It is not true though. Creativity is not magic, not uncontrollable and doesn't strike like a sudden lightning - you actually can develop it like a skill!

Creativity degrades since the times you were a child.

You can re-learn it by getting back to your roots.

Do you remember what exactly you loved doing when you were a kid?

A great artist Picasso said:

"Every child is an artist! The problem is to remain an artist when we grow up"

Einstein agreed about having fun:
"Creativity is intelligence having fun"

Creativity is an outcome of your ambitions. It is based on your ability to process the art and science of ideas and execute your vision.

What influences creativity?

It is starts with you having fun, followed by your passions, how positive and driven you are about it.

Idea development and exact creation of your new business will then need you to be persistent in execution.

Typical creative process involves the following:

1: Knowing where you are now and accumulation of necessary knowledge about what you want (your goals or aspirations)

2: Ideation

3: Idea development

4: Validation and preparation for the implementation

It loops back to the start and normally never stops even when you have an existing business.

Let's get back to ideation process in ancient times one more time.

Three greatest men - Socrates, Plato and Aristotle regarded it as a divine process, however the key value was seen in *analysis*, *judgment* and *argument*.

Whilst analytical approach is very beneficial, it doesn't provide tools to actually create something.

Creative design process learns how to use the results of analysis to actually 'construct' or 'build' something.

Design process involves the steps that can be easily employed by any startup:
you start with a definition of the problem, then do some research about it,
you start to ideate, then implement it and finish with a learning phase (loop back).
See, it is the same as creativity.

Business books are teaching you the rules with the aim to guide you through the entrepreneurial path.

Yet there is no single path!

This book moves on to outline the tools for idea generation and aims to make it fun! The rest is up to you.

This quest for new ideas is to find one's happiness, should you wish to share your feedback, please get in touch by ideas@eviljoy.com!

So what exactly is **new business** or **start-up**?

It is an initiative focused on *growth*, includes *risks* and financial *rewards*, is *scalable* and potentially aims for *market leadership*. (Please note that there are exceptions, i.e. lifestyle or side businesses)

Why it is important?

Starting a new business now is like buying a new home. We all have the freedom and assets to create a prosperity we want, to shape our lives the way we want.

Our assets are in ourselves: these are our gifts, passions, goals and efforts.
Remember, the best idea will come based on your assets.
This whole book and set of exercises are based on that.

Your idea is based on you and your:

.

- **skills**
  (always improve your expertise!);

- **creative processes**
  (find some more techniques in this book!);

- **motivation**
  (do you realise why are you doing this?);

- **social environment**
  (engage, communicate, share).

Ready to explore?

Are you thinking about a risk of failure and start fearing the consequences?

You can have a look at the additional 'Overcoming fears' article, but the main issue here is to learn how to fail correctly (be prepared), yet to be bold with your plans.

Let's agree that your only fear should be about missing the right idea!

Moving on our exploratory journey.
Let's discuss who those famous entrepreneurs are.
They play different roles,
but four definite ones are:

1. **As an Explorer** they will seek and shape opportunities.

2. **As an Artist** they will generate new ideas, options and alternatives.

3. **As a Judge** they will evaluate and select the right idea.

4. And finally as a **Warrior** they need to be able to implement that idea well.

Do you see how it also linked with the design process described above? I.e. you need to become a damn good warrior to execute brilliantly.

As it is all within you, what do you need to succeed?

Experts state the following personal qualities to be of help: stamina, commitment, ability to bounce back and be cheerful, motivation to excel, opportunity perception, tolerance of risk and uncertainty.

One of the key factors is your **optimism**.

It drives you to seek opportunities and explore further when others would give up. It leads you to make judgments based mostly on more positive factors and discount uncertainties. You also perceive less risk when being optimistic.

Your skills and passions are the key assets for your idea.

You are looking at your **mastery**!

Being a master of a skill or interest and learning or improving constantly allows you to experience incremental successes on your way to having a great business idea.

OK, why after so many great optimistic keywords there is evil in this joy?

Sociologist Fisher noted that 'the evil and the good evolve simultaneously', it is like good and bad, satisfied needs and unmet wants, being impulsive and rational.

Ask yourself a question now - *Is there anyone who needs to give you permission to start*?

Harness the power of doing something now! As all you need is enthusiasm, big vision and also some stubbornness not to be stopped by critics.

Before we go further with idea generation tools, what can you do just now?

Nurture the idea seeds! Those are your glimpses of ideas, parts that are everywhere. You encounter it without actually logging it in your memory, on paper or as notes (i.e. at your EvilJoy.com account). Collect and come back to them, they will motivate you and trigger your imagination later on. They need to work together, mingle with each other, connect and form something new.

Cultivate hunches by simply going for a walk, write your hunches down, keep the notes messy, take on several hobbies, go for a drink and build a big depository of **idea seeds**. If it helps, disconnect from your social media accounts or even mobile phone and get going!

CHAPTER 2. BEFORE THE STORM

'Imagination rules the world' © Napoleon

'The faculty of imagination is the great spring of human activity, and the principle source of human improvement'
© Dugold Stewart (Scottish philosopher)

With this pre-idea generation chapter let's move from abstract entrepreneurs and creativity concepts directly to You!

Einstein once said that 'I have no special talents, I am only passionately curious'.

Can you think straightaway if there is something that you are so passionately curious about?
It normally engages your mind so much it sparks!
What is it?

Why it is so important?

Simply because you should not waste time and live somebody else's life!

During this whole 'Me' exercise take notes, create a swap file using your note taking app, fancy planner or at EvilJoy.com which you can access online or on-the-go and use your Notes section.

You can record your night dreams there, but also copy quotes and clippings, ads, notes, links etc. Nurture your future ideas.

Start this journey with getting to know what you enjoy doing.

It is not about re-invention: it is just a very honest truth about what really matters to you. Be brutally honest with yourself and you get the starting point right!

Entrepreneurs should be aware of who they are (values, tastes) and what they know (expertise, knowledge, experience, skills).

To continue this exercise, make a list of something you really *do not want to do.*

Without looking at the below, just create this initial a no-go list.

Then slightly reverse your thinking and identify the opposites of these worst cases.

Another exercise that you will love is about having a break and naming it 'YOUR' day, so only doing stuff you like.

When on 'your' day, think about how unique you are.

It is about a competitive advantage of your inner self - what skills and passions are making you a unique individual?

Questions are an integral part of discovering something new. Ask them!

Become your own therapist! What sort of things you fill your head with? What do you read? Do you subscribe to anything? Be honest and open about the things you like.

There is no guilt in your pleasures!

Make a list of your current sources - what do you read on the web, buy magazines, watch TV..

Start being enthusiastic about this 'Me' discovery process.

What do you wish for? Your wishes also tend to inspire ideas.

Remember it is not all the time about the complexity of your ideas - experts agree that a lot of success to be found with simple ideas that are fantastically well implemented.

Are those fears creeping in again?

Analyze them: is it a fear of choice (we always decide on something neutral, just not to fail!) or a fear of judgment (others may say something awful, but think about it - ideas are just yours!)?

Become fearless by trying this exercise: Imagine you would never fail, can you now write down your thoughts about things you will do?

A. Palmer said
"The harder I practice the luckier I get".

Work, ideate and be prepared to anticipate opportunities. You can create your own luck, because being in the right place at the right time is just being in the right state of mind.

This state of mind can be found in networks; your ideas will float, mingle spillover and converge in them.

You also get smarter when connected to a network. It creates an environment where different ideas can connect to each other and develop into something meaningful for you.

In example, EvilJoy.com is one of such networks aiming to help with the ideas' flow.
It is like a dating service for promising hunches.
It is easier to disseminate ideas, but also to complete ideas!

So what happens when you are connected?

Remember Darwin and the survival of the fittest? These ideas will connect and compete with each other. They basically reinvent themselves by crossing conceptual borders (make a note to check boundary hopping techniques in the next chapters of this book).

You should consider to widen your networks and connect with people you are not normally surrounded with
(it gives a powerful novelty factor).

To compete with others in your chosen industry you need to add something else from other fields. At the end of the day, most new ideas are only extensions and combinations
of an existing knowledge. Don't you think?

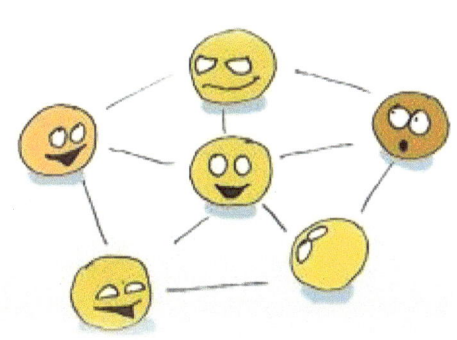

Extend yourself into different and unfamiliar areas of knowledge and practice, consider extending into your discomfort zones.

That's where you will find interesting ideas that will inspire you.

This scanning needs to become more of a habit.

Your creativity should have a purpose
and some clear restrictions
(which could be your clear wants and needs).

What it will do for you is that purpose motivates
and provides answers why you do that particular
thing, and the restrictions add some urgency to it.
Example with EvilJoy.com project: there is a
strong belief that that society rich in
entrepreneurship and innovation will be beneficial
for all of us.

Remember, ideas flow better without judgement,
the latter will just inhibit you. You never come up
with anything original if you are not prepared to
be wrong. Stop judging and just do it.

We all have ideas, many of them; yet inspiration
expires. Start doing it today. Inspiration is
magical!

CHAPTER 3. USEFUL TECHNIQUES AND EXERCISES

Hopefully you have already got a clearer idea of your:

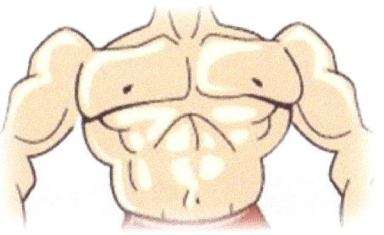

capabilities

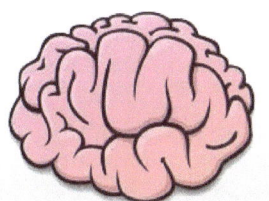

knowledge

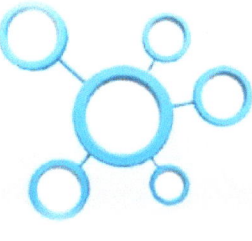

connections

financial assets

benefits
from your reputation and
past work experiences

commitments

passion for a specific
market or field

This is a base for your research as the exercises below will use your own insigns about what you really want to do. It will stimulate inspiration.

There would be both Evil, Penguin and Robin in you so listen carefully to your own self!

Are you writing ideas on napkins?
Find some time to get your notes all together
(use notes apps, planner, or EvilJoy.com notes).
If it gets complicated think about creating a visual
map (mindmap apps are widely available).

First of all, let's start with something brand new.
Sourcing inspiration from unfamiliar
is a great way to stimulate your thinking process.
Seek stimulus material in the form of pictures,
visuals, audio. Think of attending modern art
exhibitions or even musicals.
Find some new things to do.

You are already an **expert** in something.
What is it? (don't forget to write down your
thoughts as a result of the exercises)
Imagine a perfect conversation when you are
confident about the subject and enjoying it.
What is it?

When exactly you felt inspired?
Think of several subjects like this - these could be the initial ideas.
Document them - this is so called low hanging fruit, something obvious.
You can then work and dig deeper from these points.
Your aim here is to move beyond what staring you in the face.

Try the inspiration game: think about someone who inspired you. Who is that? What do they do?

Think about your own achievements. Would you be able to write a short article describing your success? This will help you to find out what exactly makes you inspired.

Brainstorm is a largely overused term.
Think about generating a lot of ideas,
the wilder the better, and you have it!

It is indeed important to remain bold and actually
generate ideas that have a chance to fail.
Those will be truly ambitious and daring!

At this point just make a long list of those daring and bold ideas. Go for a quantity.

Try a role-playing game : imagine yourself as a chef.
Think about an idea and then add something to it, then remove something. Change its colour, shape, size and design by varying and re-arranging the 'materials' (components of your idea).

Continue thinking about a chef's job: substitute components of your idea, combine some of them together. Something isn't working properly? Adapt it or eliminate. Can you put some elements to other uses?

Idea generation is like a castle you used to create on the beach.
Reduce some elements, eliminate a few, create a lot of new ones, raise standard to important ones*.

*adapted from Harvard Business Review, Chan Kim / R. Mauborgne

You can see that castle building is a great fun! Playfulness helps ideas.
Try 'Plussing' and 'Humour' techniques. They are based on improvisation. Try simulating a conversation about your ideas, where your 'opponent' needs to start his conversation with "Yes, and.." agreeing on your statement, but adding something new.

You need to pick up from that and continue. Add humour to the ideas.
What will you get as a result?

What other things chefs do?
They learn more about their passion
in front of the others and then share it.
Based on the ideas you've already taken, and your
identified passions, can you think of what is not
shared? Could it be your niche?

Simplify!
It is an easy exercise
of trying to improve your hobbies.
What can be done so you enjoy your life better?
Simplify some processes or products and other
people will like it too!

Robin always wants to make the world a bit better. Can you be of any help?

To start your 'changing the world' thinking process
going, just look for the problems that can be
automated. What could be the next big thing like
online banking or online grocery shopping?

No problem? Create a problem and automate!

After being a chef for a day,
go even further and try another good exercise:
create a children story about your hobbies.

Act like a kid, use kid's language creatively,
benefit from children simplicity and eventually
you will un-inhibit yourself!

Now, get your creative juices ready for a 'Mix and Match' exercise.

De Bono suggested that you can use some hobbies or interests to increase attractiveness of others.

So what you are going to do is to choose a hobby (say, fashion) you want to base your business idea upon and then try to increase its attractiveness by adding other hobbies or interests (i.e. sport) to it. What are you getting?

Generate a few alternatives.

Think about how Google search works - it solves a problem by using keywords. Could you do the same?

Take 4 keywords depicting your hobbies, passions and interests. Take 5 minutes to generate as many ideas as possible per each keyword.

Now you have got the ideas list. Do you like it? Are there any new items in it?

Can you try and check how one idea can be merged with another to create even a better one? Try merging them until really stuck. What do you get? Make a list.

Get cozy on your sofa and try to reflect a little bit. How exactly do your hobbies and interests link to existing businesses? Are those businesses successful? Can you think of how to make one (or several) of them better?

Break and Build exercise is a powerful tool.
You may want to spend some time with it.
When constructing your ideas from passions,
break your interests down to smaller parts.

Build something new out of those smaller parts.

In example, think about food, it breaks to
shopping, cooking, serving, etc.

Break each one of them into smaller and then
build the blocks.

Finish this exercise by moving into opposite
direction: your hobbies are also a part of
something else, so combine them with the aim of
increasing the value.
What have you got at the end?

Let's move forward to something even more
powerful. There is a big opportunity in harnessing
the power of doing good.
Research has shown that most people are
becoming increasingly happy when doing good to
strangers.

Think about your hobbies and how useful they are to other people.
Can you make them useful? It is an interesting challenge how to turn your passion
into something meaningful for other people.

The need of human contact.

Imagine rugby.
The ball is the idea, pass it on, talk to people.
Play with the balls and ideas
will be born during or after that contact.
It is important to start discussing your preliminary
or even very young ideas with other people as you
may have get a valuable question which will spark
more ideas in that direction.

Telling people about your idea is not an easy thing.
Think of creating a story about it,
use your interests and hobbies as keywords.

What is missing, what would you like to add to the
story so it shines and describes your dreams better?

Try another approach to storytelling.

You are at the start of your new business journey,
imagine the end of it. Define it - is it a successful
restaurant (1 or 2 stars?), a business that you've
just sold?

What you need to do now is to sketch the middle
part, what happened before the success? What do
you need to do to get to the imagined end.

You can also play a game of making up a story with your friends, so each one of you is telling this story to others.

Give yourself and your friends a set of characters, emotions and settings. Try to use different drafts of business ideas to make it very close to the point. Random selection of one character - one emotion - one setting will give a background for a story. Tell your friends about it!

OK, we have had a few games and enteractive exercises done. Let's get a bit analytical. Where exactly can you search for opportunities?

First of all, look at areas which are unexpected, sort of unfamiliar to you (include the ones you know a lot about as well).

To continue, think about which processes can be improved. I.e. is that particular business currently offering a delivery service?

What about demographic changes.

UK market is getting increasingly old. Do you know how to use this fact?

Browse the press and Internet to spot significant changes in a given industry or your chosen market, follow the trends and emerging technologies. Get the new knowledge working for you.

Think about your unmet needs, is there something you would like to change (and offer)?

A word about restrictions. They were mentioned earlier on. What they do is trigger your creativity to find a solution. Play a challenge game: make a list of things, or activities or negative things (in your hobbies) that you do not want. Now make a list of actions how to over come them. Are those actions forming into some sort of business opportunity?

You now see that these restrictions can trigger serious innovation. What is it and what are the approaches to innovation?

- Identify a problem and seek a solution
- Identify a solution and seek a problem
- Identify a need and seek a solution

You should have quite a list of preliminary ideas now.
It is time to tap into the power of alternatives. Different alternatives or even different ideas create convergence - ideas bump into each other and create amazingly unpredictable results. It is simple, but beautiful. Let's illustrate.

Here goes an example on simple convergence from Startups magazine - "One day I was listening to the music through a pair of headphones that i had a black shoelace-like cord rather than plastic, Benedetto recalls. My iPhone was sitting on my desk and plugged into my computer with the stock white cable. I wondered to myself why there weren't more unique cables for iPhones the way there are for headphones."
Here is how it was born.

Why is it such a power?
The point of developing a lot of initial ideas lies with the fact that chance is all about numbers. There would be a lot of opportunities in your area of expertise, you should combine and get the most successful out. Some call it brainstorm, or luck, or eureka, but it doesn't matter - your success is.

Let's try another interesting tool.
Relevance crossing is about looking at your wildest ideas. Was there something you felt just a bit 'too much' or 'unrealistic'? Come back to it and explore how irrelevant they actually are. Are they? Could they be tweaked a little?

Remember how good is networking for you? To illustrate the spillover and connections let's try this exercise. Let's call it 'the adjacent one'. Start with your passion and draw a map of adjacent territories (get creative, think about plenty of choices - your passions and interests are somehow connected).

Every connection is potentially a different business opportunity.
Work on a combination of these second tier branches (connections) and you would see something entirely new emerging from your initial set.
You can start checking how interesting those connections are.

As an option you may want to try and combine second and further tiers from different sets of passions to form an idea. What would you get? Generate different options and play with the importance factor of how passionate you are about those ideas to determine strong links and eliminate occasional unimportant ones (you can simply discard those)

It has been a lot of hard work. Have a break, a drink and chilled out time and just play a relaxing 'Dream game': write up a few sentences about your own dream. Anything really. Nobody's watching!

Consider how a journalist will write about your success story in 5-10 years time? What did you achieve and how? What was a secret?

(compare your 'dreams' with 'achievements' exercise earlier on, do you think this became more daring and bold?)

Remember the notes about being useful?
One simple way how to do it
is just to focus on selling happiness!
Develop ideas that give happiness to people.

Gift giving is a powerful 'happiness' tool.
What would you create to give others as a gift?

A note about execution: "if you never have a single great idea in your life but became skilled in executing great ideas of others, you can succeed beyond your wildest dreams. Seek them out and make them work. They do not have to be your ideas. Execution is all in this regard." Felix Dennis (How to get rich).

Novelty is a factor you should not focus entirely. If you figure out what exactly you would love to do, it can be an existing idea, yet your task is to make it work perfectly!

You have a list of ideas. You have probably thought about which are in your short list. Your brain is now bombarded with the questions like whether to go part time or full time, whether you are being realistic, various money and funding concerns.

These questions can block your brainstorm and creativity though. It is a challenge, but you need to let it go for a while and simply feel free to brainstorm, you will cope with the issues later when you have your great business idea. Why to worry in advance?

CHAPTER 4. FOCUS IT!

Your initial idea is unpolished.
As you work on your idea, the long term vision should be appearing from the initial sparkle and fog.

As most authors agree, the ingenious idea almost never springs into people's minds fully formed. They also add that when you describe it, try to make features of your idea to be mostly descriptive and benefits to be mostly emotional.

There are a few shaping techniques. Kawasaki's 'The art of the start' techniques are very helpful.

First of all, you need to make a meaning. Whatever it may be - make the world a better place, increase a quality of life, maybe even right a terrible wrong, or prevent the end of something good.

Example: if EvilJoy.com never existed the world would be worse off because there would be less entrepreneurs inspired to achieve something and live their lives as they want to.

Attempt to make a matra.
It can be something simple and catchy to describe your idea or business.
Example: EvilJoy.com is about ideas.
Fun and easily generated.

Just do it.
You need to remember to get going. It is not just about being persistent, but you also should think big, it is good if your project will polarise people, it will most certainly get you some soul mates. Play with different designs, be it packaging or product itself, find a better way to do certain things (even small things, like efficient accounting, software will do!).

Think about your business model: be specific with it, try to simplify it, if stuck at some point, start to copy what works and get creative juices flowing later on.
Finally, at this stage define some milestones (ask friends, validate idea, raise capital, make a real test and achieve breakeven - see more in the chapters to follow) and break them down to specific tasks (that you can easily follow and execute).

Start creating a clear prototype for our idea. This is an overused word, if your product is not physical, or it is very difficult to make a prototype just describe it in a very great detail.

Remember your restrictions from the previous chapters? What exactly are those? M. Meyer (at that time an employee of Google) said that 'The constraints shape and focus problems, provide clear challenges to overcome'.

It is time for a new game: try a 'Fame interview', when you imagine you have achieved your goal and give an interview to a well known journalist (media).
What would you say? Take notes.

Another good idea at this point would be to assess your idea.

Ask yourself whether you feel pleasant inside, inspired about it?

Is it something that you love? Do you think you will help people and get recognised for that? Have you thought about how much time you can dedicate to it? Can you do it full-time or require a more gradual part-time approach? Do you have your own savings to fund the initial step or you have a partner? Have you thought about anyone who can help in the beginning, maybe freelancers?

The previous chapter asked you to delay your worries and concerns,
but this is the time for you to be realistic about the prospects.
Check your inspiration again. At the end if you are not inspired, it is not **your** thing!

Let's switch off and play a new game. It is now about advertisement.
This is your time to shine and show your idea to the world by creating an ad for it. Write it down, shape it until you are happy with it. It will help to focus on what is important.

Focus on the BIG IDEA. - do not allow to have many options within a selected one, go for the main one and focus on it.

Sell happiness!
You saw in the previous chapters that it is important to focus on getting people happy, can you say that your idea lives up to that expectation?

Have a look at this checklist and do a simple screening:

- how good the idea solves the problem (with the defined purpose and restrictions);
- how novel is the solution?
- how attractive your market and industry are?
- how your mission and aspirations are connected to the idea?
- are you able to execute?
- can you make money out of your target segment? is the production cost or other expenditures lower than the projected profit?
- with all points checked do you have a sustainable advantage, so you can plan long-term?

Keep on going with shaping your idea.
Play a game and take an imaginary pill (no, just an imaginary one please!):
can you describe your idea or company as a painkiller?

Some entrepreneurs noted that your new business should not look like a vitamin, but more of a very effective painkiller.
NB. It is a very visually stimulating exercise, but of course if your vitamin-alike business idea still gets a very good response from a screening stage and you are very driven to go for it, who are they to tell you to stop?

This painkilling effect is your area of strength - focus on it!

Continuing with the popular practices it is also well-known to have a 'daunting session' when you imagine a 'Near death experience'. Yes, it is tough, but very effective to focus yourself on the things that matter!

To finish your shaping practice, you can test it. You can go on and sell this to yourself. Make sure that you are going to make something that you are prepared to buy yourself. It is very probable that others will buy that too (and vice versa). Now let's move forward and get to those 'others' who matter.

CHAPTER 5. ASK FRIENDS

The question you can ask yourself at this stage is whether 'my idea is viable'?

Many people are afraid to go and open up about it. There is a clear benefit of getting an idea out. When you have this precious 'light bulb moment': flesh the idea out, gather feedback, give the idea some definition and momentum.

Check how your friends and then in the next chapter the whole world connect with your plans and prospects.

According to a research, the biggest barrier for a person not to discuss the idea with their friends would be their fear of a defeat. Yet you should be confident enough to at least present this to our friends, otherwise why to pursue it if you have no inner confidence?

Involve your friends to evaluate the idea and use their inputs. This is an invaluable work how to deal with the arguments: will they break your idea or make it stronger?

Now it is their turn to say whether they will buy it from you.

Ask them whether there is a real need for that.
Listen to their reactions.
Discover the value of getting out to the world and asking as many questions as you can.
Start with your friends and then skip to the next chapter and ask the world!

People can still be very cautious. Why is it important to share ideas instead of keeping it all to yourself? Is it also very risky?
The major argument is that creativity needs a network and some sort of social environment. You can work in a group to have more options and alternatives. You are learning new things by simply asking, sharing, creating and executing.

Sometimes we need that feedback from friends, yet they are unavailable or busy (and we are all quite impatient!).

There is a solution though and it is to make it public to a group of people who live the same thought (entrepreneurial spirit, you name it). They are all looking to find out how to make their interests (or passions) a viable business.

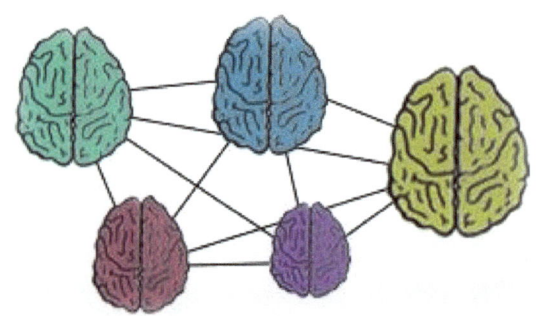

Chance favours the connected mind.

CHAPTER 6. EXTERNAL VALIDATION

After the previous chapter, it is important to do almost the same, but with the wider group of people. Ask strangers whether there is a real need for the idea. Even the most powerful ideas may get negative reaction from the experts. Yet you can use their inputs of why this won't work for your new idea design.

As a preparation for this stage it will help you to craft the sales pitch!

The best ideas are coming out through impromptu, thought-provoking chats. Talk it out and connect.

It is what researchers call a focus group. It helps to understand actual behaviours (i.e. of your future customers). It became really simple nowadays - you can create online questionnaires, make a poll or invite people for Skype or Hangouts interviews.

Are you starting to fear a potential judgement? It is a usual reaction to getting your idea fully out to the world, yet remember, each one of us can have a very different understanding of what makes a good idea.

Get help with questions.

You can make your project more interactive by prompting people to write stimulus (basically questions about your business) and give/get feedback.
Peter Sims in his book 'Little Bets' said that 'Entrepreneurial plans and made and unmade, followed upon through action and interaction with others'.

Society tends to keep ideas in chains. Yet the state of happiness, or 'flow' as described by M. Csikszentmihalyi is achieved when you are connected and inspired.

Keep in mind that when you go network-wide seeking for free innovation, you would also need a screening mechanism to get rid of some junk along the way.

Poincare said that 'Ideas rise in crowds' - in the modern world they rise in the so called 'liquid networks' where the connection is valued more than protection. See Steven Johnson 'Where good ideas are coming from' for more information on liquid networks.

Another brilliant author Austin Kleon added that 'The more you give away, the more comes back to you'. It is not that he was the first to mention that, the term of 'karma' is an ancient one, yet it is so true with regards to getting the idea to be fully shaped.

Happiness, entrepreneurship and karma
seem to be interchangeable terms here, don't you think?

At this point you can start thinking now about how to turn your external connections into partnerships. Ben Way said
'In business people around you matter a lot'.

It is about you to make a huge benefit from your network. You really should start seeking partners pro-actively at this stage.

CHAPTER 7. THE POWER OF PARTNERSHIPS

What is your perfect team?

A visionary (you?)

A designer

A Marketing and Sales dude

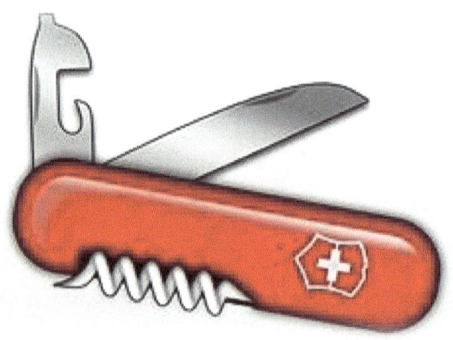

An army knife to get it all done
(great exec)

A wise and experienced mentor?

Johann Wolfgang von Goethe, who also wrote 'Faust', once said that 'whatever you can do or dream you can, begin it. Boldness has genius, power and magic in it. Begin it now'.

Think about the question of what exactly you should be responsible for or more interested in doing, and what you are prepared to delegate.

Delegation can be easy for some people, yet most of us find it very difficult to trust others. In most cases you would need to learn that skill, as in example IT is normally a very complex discipline and outsourcing is almost inevitable.

You are setting your own business, but it also means setting up rules for yourself! It constitutes some sort of a challenge and a conflict, but also an increased freedom for yourself!

Chesborough underlined the power of partnerships by saying that 'open innovation is sourcing ideas outside, where links and connections become more important than ownership of knowledge'.

CHAPTER 8. SEEK MATERIAL (FINANCIAL) RESOURCES.

Reaching this point, you would get a more or less clear understanding of your idea(s) and an outline or hopefully a quite firm description.

You have an abundance of books about raising the capital, so feel free to shop around and search the web. This was about your ideation process, not financing! Yet the most obvious ways of raising finance now are:

- Bank loans (some banks are increasingly focusing on startups and offer quite attractive schemes)
- Your friends and family may be convinced by your idea and want to invest
- Angel investors (in most cases they will require your business to be already set up and probably show some performance, so it is more suited for growing businesses, but there were cases of funding the startups so it is worth exploring)
- Partners (partnerships could be beneficial not only from the aspect of business involvement, but also from financial perspective when your partner(s) will buy a share and invest a needed amount)

There would be additional questions of going small or aggressive, etc. The answer should be found by analysing what strategy will bring you to achieve your goal (taking into account your set restrictions, i.e. minimum risks), taking it into consideration with your business plan.

CHAPTER 9. PRELIMINARY BUSINESS PLAN

They say you need to think big, start small and grow fast. Challenge what exactly is fast in your case.

Think about 5 major challenges to your idea. Create a list of actions how to overcome those. This would shape your business plan.

Define what would you deem as a success.

Have a look at business planning resources, they are widely available online, including on EvilJoy.com

10. MAKE TESTS AND PROTOTYPES

 Compare your tests with what you have set as the exact success measure. Do they meet your expected results? If not, make your idea better.

CHAPTER 11. DEVELOP. EXECUTE. JUST DO IT

Ok, well, let's admit - we all fear and we all think about our risks.
How do you feel about a vivid risk of not following your dream though?

Experts are united in one hard truth - if you have ideas or just one good idea you still won't get paid a penny for just being a superior visionary. You need to implement it with excellence; staring at your brilliant idea won't get you anywhere.

Be authentic and relevant.
Richard Branson also said that you should not be greedy in your execution. If you are making yourself useful, do it; money would come.

Idea is like a guitar - it doesn't mean a thing unless you know how to use it.

Look back at your initial problem and check with yourself whether this developed idea of yours corresponds to what you wanted to solve initially. Start challenging thoughts and opinions until you have a firm confidence.

Take it one day at a time.
It is clear that you will start working almost 24/7 with your idea. Slow down a little, have a rest, a good sleep, well you know what to do to make yourself happy (just outside of this project!) Restart in a new day with an increased energy and drive.

Just to throw you a kicking question - do you want a quiet and predictable life?

What are your ambitions when thinking about your idea? Do you think big enough and talking to many people?

Avoid a burnout and recharge. Do not forget to have a break, you did that to get more creative juices flowing, but it is also important whilst in the execution phase. Get inspired again by going on a holiday, or simply disconnect from everything for a short while.

Your area of expertise should be kept relevant and up-to-date. Don't be content with your mastery, learn constantly.

CHAPTER 12. EVILJOY.COM STORY

We invite you to an optional detour of how we came to our EvilJoy.com idea. We wrote a script to that drama, but there is no final point. You create a destination for yourself!

Hey there, Joy's here!

Please allow me to tell you about my journey to here and hopefully give you some ideas how you can get going on yours!

Funny enough, but you are going to shape our story as well
(being a very active idea generator and collaborator!).

My friends Robin and Penguin with my humble self are committed to help you to turn your passions into new business ideas.
It all began for us in early April 2013...

I have a great job that I enjoy.

It has been already quite some time since I knew that I'd like something more in addition to what I do. The question was 'what?' - or how to do something I truly love and earn from it?

I have tried though - you normally start with something that is obvious and easy, probably something close to what you do now.

Yet I found it very difficult to keep on doing almost the same job (for myself) I was doing at work.

Sounds familiar?

The most important thing for me was to find an answer to that question that would also inspire me most of the time!

Shall I say I consider myself quite a proactive evil?

I guess it was a time to think differently and consider this frustration as actually an opportunity to shake things up (mwahaha)

The search has started!

It has been one book after another, long hours working on my laptop researching. It has been actually quite boring and tiring at times.

How to approach this? What is it going to be?

Yeah.. it is going nowhere..

I consider myself as creative,
I was told I was a good friend and quite knowledgeable...

Speaking about friends.. Hello, Robin!

R (after hearing me out): I am actually happy to do what I love, it is such a hard work, but I definitely know why I wake up every morning, commute to the meetings..

Alright, more books then?

More research?

How can you keep yourself alive
with these piles of books?

Hello my uni friend! (We call him Penguin.. shhh...
no wonder why!)

P: 'Success is 1% inspiration and 99% perspiration'
as said by T. Edison

Penguin reminded me to look how it was done
earlier, the cliche tales told me to try something
that helped in the past!

We all know about these
'idea generation techniques'.

(impatiently waiting for a spark of brilliance) Is it going to happen?

No?

What exactly did that Penguin say about Edison and his ideas?

Again nothing?

Do I do something wrong?

58

How can I force the ideas out?

It has been dozen of 400p books, another dozen of 300p and nothing! It is also supposed to be fun and exciting (bliss of discovery or something!), yet it became just boring to read almost the same story over and over again...

To tell the truth I have been putting something down on paper but it was just left there. I do not think I am confident enough it would work!

R: Just imagine a day, or no, better a week of sheer fun!

Oh that can be nice!

R: not just that you naughty one!

After some time I am sure you would eventually
turn to do something..
What would it be?

Shhh, don't disturb the party!

It has been quite fun, quite..

Ok it is enough! That fun doesn't excite me
anymore, it was quite meaningless and started to
be boring too. Am I that helpless?

People say you need to be thinking about helping others, that's a very positive thought.

What do I already know? Wine.. that's just a hobby, isn't it? I can do gambling, it is so evil!

This search is starting to look like a big gamble as well. Can I do writing? Is that evil enough?

One day I have received a call from a friend.

One of the things she asked me as to help her with some optimisation idea with regards to her online store. I think I was very drawn into that and gave her a good advice, she seemed to be very happy! It felt very good and definitely a time well spent.

After a short while my telephone rang and I've got a very good feedback from her: 'Thanks mate! It was your quick glance and I was able to optimise my shop's delivery payments and improved my margin! Well done, let's have a drink when you are in town'

Ah, bless, it is very nice!

She rang me afterwards: 'Hey, I've just thought that I would share my new business idea with you - you seem to grasp quickly the new things and I also wanted to discuss it with somebody...'

It was not a flash or eureka moment - it just came to me naturally - it was something I would love to do.

It also felt right - time started to pass so quickly, I do enjoy dealing with ideas, the novelty factor and I am also able to help others!

Let me dig deeper into that subject.

(I knew I was really passionate about this all. In addition to that my own business career indicates I'm actually very good dealing with new business)

Asking questions helps.

Thing is, I need more people to give me feedback. I need to make sure my idea is viable.

Do you think some of them can become my partners for this project?

Friends: Euh, we are not sure, but let's get in touch and we get you connected to other entrepreneurs as well - it is a big chance that there would be someone who would love you idea.

They would like to discuss things with you and potentially get involved.

I went on to ask people I know...

I can help. Tell me!

I will also connect you with people I know!

I can help too - I have a broad knowledge of online retail.

Huh? Where do start I?

The idea is just so young and fragile now. I can see some small parts of it, but I need more help!

You should ask them whether they are willing to provide feedback or maybe even contribute to it somehow.

There are some who definitely should have some knowledge like Penguin does.

My friend told me that she felt that feedback could potentially shape her idea better than any advice she gets from the books.

I understood why other people kept on saying about the 'power of networks'.

Awesome! It sounds like fun!

How about I will research, collect and share some useful information on idea generation, new business, startups, and entrepreneurship?

Go for it! I will try to help you make it fun! Fun THINK-ing!

Joy, your fun is addictive!
I am now thinking that the materials about
entrepreneurship should be straight
to the point, but also visually stimulating.

(about helping a friend with the knowledge and
idea feedback) You know guys it seems like we
might just have our first 'client'!

Let's help her with her idea - it is still very sketchy
and young. She needs more people to make it
work...

For example, we should help her to find potential
partners or collaborators...

Or just simply gain confidence, traction and momentum for her idea

Getting this young and fragile ideas off the ground for the first time is so important - without it the idea just stays in her mind or at most on paper..

Sounds lovely!

She should be able to log all tiny aspects of her idea in one place and keep on developing it.

She doesn't know what this idea would turn out to be at the end (from those small details and parts), but it is such fun as it can turn out to be much more than she expected it to be!

She asked me how much would we charge for it?

We will publish her idea for free to get our service moving as well!

Erm, hold on a second - we should cover our costs and then earn a little as well!

Agreed, but I will work extra to support all socially responsible ideas and they would go public for free.

OK, we will need to charge for the published Public idea and the creator will have all the functionality except adding attachments or URLs to it.

For the latter we would need additional resources so the Premium should be at extra charge.

(we need to research the market now and check the competition) Looks competitive

Guys, it seems that my passion actually represents a business idea about new business ideas of others.

How cool!

Awww, congrats mate! I didn't have any doubts you will succeed!

Do not forget to do good things and help people!

Stop for a second, you! Let's protect idea's privacy though! People should be in control of the visibility of the ideas.

OK! Consider it done. People should switch on and off the visibility at any time and also be able to edit ideas and comments at any time!

EvilJoy should open its doors to fun ideas in Gaming, Art, Food and Drink, Creative Media, Sport, and Other entertaining ones.

Turn your passions into new business ideas we say!

Welcome and enjoy our THINK section of exclusive content, browse and get involved into all ideas in SHARE section, the PLAY and GIVE ones are dedicated to the ideas in Gaming or socially responsible ones backed by Robin respectively. EnJoy!

BIBLIOGRAPHY

- Larry Keeley et al "Ten Types of Innovation", Wiley, 2013, USA
- Austin Kleon "Steal Like an Artist", Workman publishing company, 2012, USA
- Austin Kleon "Show Your Work", Workman publishing company, 2014, USA
- Hugh Macleod "Freedom is Blogging in Your Underwear", Portfolio / Penguin, 2012, USA
- Chris Garden and Catherine Blackburn "Employee to Entrepreneur", Pearson Education, 2013, UK
- Jason Fried & David Heinemeier Hansson "Rework", Vermilion, a Random House Company, 2010, UK
- Ken Robinson "The Element. How Finding Your Passion Changes Everything", Penguin Books, 2009, UK.
- Jurgen Wolff "Creativity Now", Second Edition, Pearson, 2012, UK
- Jamie Smart "Clarity", Capstone Publishing, 2013, UK
- Edward De Bono "Six Thinking Hats", Penguin Books, 2000, UK
- Sam Harrison "Ideaspotting. How to Find Your Next Great Idea", 1st ed., HOW books, 2006, USA.
- Daniel Priestley "Entrepreneur Revolution", Capstone Publishing, 2013, UK
- Scott Belsky "Making Ideas Happen", Portfolio Penguin, 2010, USA
- Peter Sims "Little Bets", Random House Business Books, 2012, UK
- Bryan W. Mattimore "Idea Stormers. How to Lead and Inspire Creative Breakthroughs", 1st ed., Jossey-Bass, 2012, USA.
- Andy Boynton, Bill Fischer "the Idea Hunter. How to Find the Best Ideas and Make them Happen", Jossey-Bass, 2012, USA
- Dave Gray, Sunni Brown, James Macanufo "Gamestorming. A Playbook for Innovators, Rulebreakers, and Changemakers", First Edition, O'Reilly, 2012, USA
- Gavin Ambrose, Paul Harris "Design Thinking", AVA Publishing SA, 2010, Switzerland
- David S. Kidder "The Startup Playbook", Chronicle Books, 2012, USA
- Matt Thomas, Shaa Wasmund "The Smarta Way To Do Business", Capstone Publishing, 2011, UK
- Mihaly Csikszentmihalyi "The Psychology of discovery and Invention", Harper Perennial Modern Classics, 2013, USA
- Mihaly Csikszentmihalyi "Flow. The classic work on how to achieve happiness", Rider, Random House Group, 2002, UK
- Alexander Osterwalder & Yves Pigneur "Business Model Generation", Weley & Sons, 2010, USA

- Bill Aulet "Disciplines Entrepreneurship", Wiley, 2013, USA
- Steve Blank and Bob Dorf "The Startup Owner's Manual", K and S Ranch Inc, 2012, USA
- Guy Kawasaki "The Art of the Start", Portfolio, Penguin Group, 2004, USA
- Sara Williams "Financial Times Guides: Business Startup 2011", Prentice Hall, 2011, UK
- David Lester "Start Your Own Business 2013", Crimson Publishing, 2013, UK
- David Burkus "The Myths of Creativity", Jossey-Bass, 2014, USA
- Dave Stewart and Mark Simmons "The Business Playground", Prentice Hall, Pearson Education, 2010, UK
- John Coleman, Daniel Gulati, W. Oliver Segovia "Passion & Purpose", Harvard Business Review Press, 2012, USA
- "Start Your Own Business", by the staff of Entrepreneur Media Inc, with foreword by Peter Shea, CEO; 5th Edition, Entrepreneur Media, 2010, USA
- John Williams "Screw Work, Let's Play", Pearson Education, 2012, UK
- Mary Bragg, Andrew Bragg "Developing New Business Ideas: A Step-by-step Guide to Creating New Business Ideas Worth Backing"., Prentice Hall, 2006, UK
- Hugh Macleod "Ignore Everybody", Portfolio, 2009, USA
- Steven Johnson "Where the Good Ideas Come From. The Seven Patterns of Innovation", Penguin Books, 2010, USA
- John Hunt "The Art of the Idea", Powerhouse Books, 2009, USA
- Hugh Macleod "Evil Plans", Marshall Cavendish Business, 2011, UK
- Peter Watson "Ideas. A History from Fire to Freud", Phoenix, 2006, UK
- Stefan Mumaw "Creative Bootcamp", New Riders, 2012, USA
- Stan Lee's "How to Write Comics", Dynamite Entertainment, 2011, USA
- Scott McCloud "Understanding Comics. The Invisible Art", William Morrow, HarperCollins Publishers, 1994, USA.